COMPOUND WORDS

COMPOUND WORDS

FREDERICK WILLIAM HAMILTON

ISBN: 978-93-5614-389-0

Published: 1918

LECTOR HOUSE

LECTOR HOUSE LLP
E-MAIL: lectorpublishing@gmail.com

**TYPOGRAPHIC TECHNICAL SERIES
FOR APPRENTICES—PART VI, NO. 36**

COMPOUND WORDS

A STUDY OF THE PRINCIPLES OF COMPOUNDING, THE COMPONENTS OF COMPOUNDS, AND THE USE OF THE HYPHEN

BY

FREDERICK W. HAMILTON, LL. D.

EDUCATIONAL DIRECTOR
UNITED TYPOTHETÆ OF AMERICA.

1918

PREFACE

THE subject of compounds is one of the most difficult of the matters relating to correct literary composition. The difficulty arises from the fact that usage, especially in the matter of the presence or absence of the hyphen, is not clearly settled. Progressive tendencies are at work and there is great difference of usage, even among authorities of the first rank, with regard to many compounds in common use.

An attempt is made to show first the general character of the problems involved. Then follows a discussion of the general principles of compounding. The general rules for the formation of compounds are stated and briefly discussed. The various components of compounds are fully analyzed and tabulated. The best modern usage in the matter of the employment of the hyphen is set forth in a series of rules. The whole is concluded by practical advice to the compositor as to the use of the rules in the actual work of the office.

CONTENTS

COMPOUND WORDS

INTRODUCTION

THE English language contains a great many words and phrases which are made up of two or more words combined or related in such a way as to form a new verbal phrase having a distinct meaning of its own and differing in meaning from the sum of the component words taken singly. *Income* and *outgo*, for example, have quite definite meanings related, it is true, to *come* and *go* and to *in* and *out*, but sharply differentiated from those words in their ordinary and general signification. We use these compound words and phrases so commonly that we never stop to think how numerous they are, or how frequently new ones are coined. Any living language is constantly growing and developing new forms. New objects have to be named, new sensations expressed, new experiences described.

Sometimes these words are mere aggregations like *automobile, monotype, sidewalk, policeman* and the like. Sometimes, indeed very often, they are short cuts. A *hatbox* is a box for carrying a hat, a *red-haired* man is a man with red hair. A *bookcase* is a case to contain books, etc.

Sometimes the phrase consists of two or more separate words, such as *well known* or *nicely kept*. Sometimes it consists of words joined by a hyphen, such as *boarding-house, sleeping-car*. Sometimes it consists of a single word formed by amalgamating or running together the components, such as *penholder, nevertheless*.

In which of these forms shall we write the phrase we speak so easily? How shall we shape the new word we have just coined? Which of these three forms shall we use, and why? Ordinarily we look for the answer to such questions from three sources, historical development, the past of the language; some logical principle of general application; or some recognized standard of authority. Unfortunately we get little help from either of these sources in this special difficulty.

The history of the language is a history of constant change. The Anglo-Saxon tongue was full of compounds, but the hyphen was an unknown device to those who spoke it. The English of Chaucer, the period when our new-born English tongue was differentiated from those which contributed to its composition, is full of compounds, and the compounds were generally written with a hyphen. Shakespeare used many compound words and phrases some of which sound strange, if not uncouth, to modern ears, but used the hyphen much less than Chaucer. In modern times the tendency has been and is to drop the hyphen. The more general progression seems to be (1) two words, (2) two words hyphenated, (3) two words run together into one. Sometimes, however, the hyphen drops, leaving two words separated. That there is constant change, and that the change is progressing consistently in the direction of eliminating the hyphen is fairly clear. This, however, does not help us much. At what stage of the process are we with regard to any given word? Which form of the process is operating in any given case?

There are no laws or principles of universal application on which we may build a consistent system of practice. Certain general principles have been laid down and will be here set forth. While they are helpful to the understanding of the subject they are not sufficiently universal to serve as practical guides in all cases. In any event they need to be supplemented by careful study of the rules for the use of the hyphen, by careful study of the best usage in particular cases, and by thorough knowledge of the style of each particular office, as will be pointed out later. Authorities and usage differ widely, and it is often difficult to say that a particular form is right or wrong.

There is no recognized standard authority. The dictionaries do not agree with each other and are not always consistent with themselves. They may always write a certain word in a certain way but they may write another word to all appearance exactly analogous to the first in another way. For example Worcester has *brickwork* and *brasswork*, but *wood-work* and *iron-work*. Webster, on the other hand, has *wood-work* and *brick-work*.

The best that the printer can do is to adopt a set of rules or style of his own and stick to it consistently. Here and there a generally accepted change, like the dropping of the hyphen from *tomorrow* and *today* will force itself upon him, but for the most part he may stick to his style. Of course, the author, if he has a marked preference, must be permitted to use his own methods of compounding except in magazine publications and the like. In such cases, when the author's work is to appear in the same volume with that of other writers, the style of the printing office must rule and the individual contributors must bow to it.

GENERAL PRINCIPLES

THREE general principles are laid down by Mr. F. Horace Teall which will be found useful, though they must be supplemented in practice by more specific rules which will be given later. They are as follows:

I   All words should be separate when used in regular grammatical relations and construction unless they are jointly applied in some arbitrary way.

> An *iron fence* means a fence made of iron. The meaning and construction are normal and the words are not compounded.

> An *iron-saw* means a saw for cutting iron. The meaning is not the same as *iron saw* which would mean a saw made of iron. The hyphenated compound indicates the special meaning of the words used in this combination.

> *Ironwood* is a specific name applied to a certain kind of very hard wood. Hence, it becomes a single word compounded but without a hyphen. Either of the other forms would be ambiguous or impossible in meaning.

II   Abnormal associations of words generally indicate unification in sense and hence compounding in form.

> A *sleeping man* is a phrase in which the words are associated normally. The man sleeps.

> A *sleeping-car* is a phrase in which the words are associated abnormally. The car does not sleep. It is a specially constructed car in which the passengers may sleep comfortably.

> A *king fisher* might be a very skilful fisherman. A *kingfisher* is a kind of bird. Here again we have an abnormal association of words and as the compound word is the name of a specific sort of bird there is no hyphen. A *king-fisher*, if it meant anything, would probably mean one who fished for kings, as a *pearl-diver* is one who dives for pearls.

III   Conversely, no expression in the language should ever be changed from two or more words into one (either hyphenated or solid) without change of sense.

> *Saw trimmer* is not compounded because there is no change in the commonly accepted sense of either word.

> *Color work* is not compounded because the word *color*, by usage common in English, has the force of an adjective, and the words are used in their accepted sense. In other languages it would be differently expressed, for example, in French it would be *oeuvre*, or *imprimerie en couleur*, *work*, or,

printing in color.

Presswork is compounded because it has a special and specific meaning. Good or bad presswork is a good or bad result of work done on a press.

Here as everywhere in printing the great purpose is to secure plainness and intelligibility. Print is made to read. Anything which obscures the sense, or makes the passage hard to read is wrong. Anything which clears up the sense and makes the passage easy to read and capable of only one interpretation is right.

INFLUENCE OF ACCENT IN COMPOUNDING

Some writers lay much stress on the influence of accent in the formation of compounds while others ignore it entirely. Accent undoubtedly has some influence and the theory may be easily and intelligibly expressed. It ought to be understood, but it will not be found an entirely safe guide. Usage has modified the results of compounding in many cases in ways which do not lend themselves to logical explanation and classification.

The general principle as stated by Mr. Teall is as follows:

When each part of the compound is accented, use the hyphen; *laughter-loving*.

When only one part is accented, omit the hyphen; *many sided*.

When the accent is changed, print the compound solid; *broadsword*. This follows the general rule of accenting the first syllable in English words.

RULES FOR THE FORMATION
OF COMPOUNDS

I   Two nouns used together as a name form a compound noun unless:

(*a*)   The first is used in a descriptive or attributive sense, that is, is really an adjective, or

(*b*)   The two are in apposition.

Various uses of the noun as an adjective, that is, in some qualifying or attributive sense are when the noun conveys the sense of:

1. "Made of;" *leather belt, steel furniture.*
2. "Having the shape, character, or quality of;" *diamond pane, iron ration, bull calf.*
3. "Pertaining to, suitable for, representing;" *office desk, labor union.*
4. "Characterized by;" *motor drive.*
5. "Situated in, and the like;" *ocean current, city life.*
6. "Supporting or advocating;" *union man, Bryan voter.*
7. "Existing in or coming from;" *Yellowstone geyser, California lemon.*
8. "Originated or made by, named for;" *Gordon Press, Harvard College.*

Placing the two nouns in apposition is much the same as using the first as an adjective.

Such compounds are generally written as two words without the hyphen, but see specific rules for use of hyphens.

II   Every name apparently composed of a plain noun and a noun of agent or verbal noun, but really conveying the sense of a phrase with suffix *er, or,* or *ing,* should be treated as a compound; *roller distribution.*

III   Possessive phrases used as specific names (generally plants) are treated as compounds.

They are hyphenated unless very common, in which case they are closed up; *crane's-bill, ratsbane.*

IV   Any phrase used as a specific name in an arbitrary application not strictly figurative is written as a compound; *blueberry, red-coat, forget-me-not.*

V   Any pair of words used as one name of which the second is a noun but the first not really an adjective should be written as a compound; *foster-brother, down-*

town, after-consideration.

As elsewhere the use of the hyphen depends largely in the familiarity of the phrase; *spoilsport, pickpocket.*

VI   Any two words other than nouns should be treated as a compound, generally solid, when arbitrarily associated as a name; *standpoint, outlook.*

VII   A name or an adjective made by adding a suffix to a proper name compounded of two words should be treated as a compound with a hyphen; *East-Indian, New-Yorker.* If the name is not inflected this rule does not apply; *East India Company, New York man.*

VIII   Any pair or series of words arbitrarily associated in a joint sense different from their sense when used separately, should be compounded; *workman-like, warlike.*

COMPONENTS OF COMPOUNDS

Compounds having the force of nouns may be made up in several ways.

1. Two nouns used in other than their natural signification; *claw-hammer*.
2. A noun and an adjective used in other than their natural signification; *great-uncle, dry-goods*.
3. A noun and an adverb; *touch-down, holder-forth*.
4. A noun and an adverb; *down-draft, flare-back*.
5. A noun and a verb; *know-nothing, draw-bar*.
6. A noun and a preposition; *between-decks*.
7. Two adjectives; *high-low, wide-awake*.
8. Two verbs; *make-believe*.
9. A verb and an adverb; *cut-off, break-up*.
10. A verb and a preposition; *to-do, go-between*.

Compounds having the force of adjectives may be made up in several ways.

1. A group of words compacted into one idea; *never-to-be-forgotten*.
2. Two adjectives; *white-hot, ashy-blue*.
3. An adjective and a participle or noun and suffix simulating a participle; *odd-looking, foreign-born, bow-legged*.
4. An adjective and a noun; *fire-new, type-high*.
5. A noun and a participle (or noun and suffix simulating a participle); *hand-printed, peace-making*.
6. An adverb and an adjective used together before a noun; *well-bred, long-extended*.
7. Two nouns used adjectively before another noun; *cotton-seed oil, shoe-sewing machine, Sunday-school teacher*.
8. An adjective and a noun used together before a noun; *civil-service examination, free-trade literature, fresh-water sailor*.
9. A verb and a noun; *John Lack-land*.

Four compounds occur with the force of verbs.

1. Two verbs; *balance-reef*.

2. A verb and a noun; *silver-plate, house-break.*
3. A verb and an adjective; *cold-press, fine-still.*
4. A verb and an adverb; *cross-examine.*

Several combinations are used with the force of adverbs.

1. Two adverbs; *upright, henceforth.*
2. A noun and an adverb; *brain-sickly.*
3. An adjective and an adverb (or compound adjective with suffix, simulating an adverb); *stout-heartedly, ill-naturedly.*
4. An adjective and a verb; *broadcast.*
5. Two nouns; *piecemeal, half-mast.*
6. A noun and an adjective; *cost-free, pointblank.*
7. A noun and a preposition; *down-stairs, above-board, offhand.*

RULES FOR THE USE OF THE HYPHEN

1. Hyphenate nouns formed by the combination of two nouns standing in objective relation to each other, that is, one of whose components is derived from a transitive verb:

well-wisher *wood-turning*

mind-reader *child-study*

office-holder *clay-modeling*

When such compounds are in very common use, and especially when they have a specific or technical meaning, they are printed solid;

typewriter *stockholder*

proofreader *copyholder*

lawgiver *dressmaker*

2. Hyphenate a combination of a present participle with a noun when the meaning of the combination is different from that of the two words taken separately; *boarding-house, sleeping-car, walking-stick.*

3. Hyphenate a combination of a present participle with a preposition used absolutely (not governing the following noun); *the putting-in or taking-out of a hyphen.*

4. As a rule compounds of *book, house, will, room, shop,* and *work* should be printed solid when the prefixed noun has one syllable; should be hyphenated when it contains two; should be printed in two separate words when it contains three or more;

handbook, notebook, story-book, pocket-book, reference book.

clubhouse, storehouse, engine-house, power-house, business-house.

handmill, sawmill, water-mill, paper-mill, chocolate mill.

classroom, lecture-room, recitation room.

tinshop, tailor-shop, carpenter shop.

woodwork, metal-work, filigree work.

Unusual combinations such as *source-book* and *wheat-mill* are sometimes hyphenated, and the hyphen is sometimes omitted for the sake of the appearance as in *school work.*

5. Compounds of *maker, dealer,* and other words denoting occupation are generally hyphenated; *harness-maker, job-printer.*

The tendency is to print these words solid when they come into very common use; *dressmaker*.

6. Hyphenate nouns when combined in an adjectival sense before the name of the same person; *the martyr-president Lincoln, the poet-artist Rosetti*.

7. Compounds of *store* are generally hyphenated when the prefix contains one syllable, otherwise not; *drug-store, fruit-store* (but *bookstore*), *provision store*.

8. Compounds of *fellow* are hyphenated; *fellow-being, play-fellow*, but *bedfellow*.

9. Compounds of *father, mother, brother, sister, daughter, parent*, and *foster* should be hyphenated when the word in question forms the first part of the compound; *father-love, mother-country, brother-officer, sister-state, daughter-cell, parent-word, foster-brother*, but (by exception) *fatherland*.

10. Hyphenate compounds of *great* in phrases indicating degrees of descent; *great-grandmother, great-great-grandfather*.

11. Hyphenate compounds of *life* and *world*; *life-history, world-influence*, but (by exception) *lifetime*.

12. Compounds of *skin* with words of one syllable are printed solid, otherwise as two separate words; *calfskin, sheepskin, alligator skin*.

13. Hyphenate compounds of *master*; *master-builder, master-stroke*, but (by exception) *masterpiece*.

14. Hyphenate compounds of *god* when this word forms the second element; *sun-god, war-god, godsend, godson*.

15. Hyphenate compounds of *half* and *quarter*; *half-truth, quarter-circle, half-title*, but on account of difference in meaning of *quarter, quartermaster, headquarters*.

16. These prefixes

ante-	*infra-*	*re-*
anti-	*inter-*	*semi-*
bi-	*intra-*	*sub-*
co-	*pre-*	*super-*
demi-	*post-*	*tri-*

are ordinarily joined to the word with which they are used without a hyphen, except when followed by the same letter as that with which they terminate or by *w* or *y*;

antechamber	*post-temporal*
antiseptic	*post-graduate*
anti-imperialistic	*prearrange*
biennial	*pre-empt*
bipartisan	*recast*
co-equal	*re-enter*

co-ordinate	*semiannual*
demigod	*subconscious*
inframarginal	*subtitle*
international	*superfine*
intersperse	*tricolor*
intramural	*co-workers*
intra-atomic	*co-yield*

Exceptions are

(*a*) Combinations with proper names or adjectives derived therefrom, and long or unusual compounds;

ante-bellum	*sister-university*
anti-license	*post-revolutionary*
anti-security	*pre-Raphaelite*
demi-relievo	*re-tammanize*

(*b*) Words in which the omission of the hyphen would alter the sense;

re-formation	*reformation*
re-cover	*recover*
re-creation	*recreation*

17. The negative prefixes *un, in, il, im,* and *a* do not take a hyphen except in very rare or artificial combinations; *unmanly, invisible, illimitable, impenetrable, asymmetrical.*

The negative prefix *non* calls for a hyphen except in very common words;

non-existent	*non-combatant*
non-interference	*nonsense*
non-unionist	*nonessential*

18. The prefixes *quasi, extra, supra, ultra,* and *pan* call for a hyphen;

quasi-historical	*supra-normal*
quasi-corporation	*ultra-conservative*
extra-mural	*Pan-Germanism*

Ultramontaine, probably because a specific party designation, is always printed solid.

19. *Over* and *under* do not ordinarily call for a hyphen; *overemphasize, underfed,* but *over-careful, over-spiritualistic.*

20. Combinations having *self* and *by* as the first element of the compound call for a hyphen; *self-evident, self-respecting, by-law, by-product,* but *selfhood, selfish,* and *selfsame.*

21. Combinations of *fold* are printed as one word if the number contains only one syllable but as two if it contains more than one;

twofold	*fifteen fold*
tenfold	*a hundred fold*

22. Adjectives formed by a noun preceding *like* do not take a hyphen if the noun is a monosyllable, except when ending in *l* or a proper noun; if the noun contains more than one syllable a hyphen should be used; *childlike, warlike, catlike, bell-like, Napoleon-like*, but (by exception) *Christlike*.

23. *Vice, elect, ex, general*, and *lieutenant* as parts of titles are connected with the chief noun by a hyphen; *vice-consul, ex-president, governor-elect, postmaster-general, lieutenant-colonel*.

24. *Today, tonight*, and *tomorrow* are printed without a hyphen.

25. In fractional numbers spelled out connect the numerator and denominator by a hyphen. "*The day is three-quarters gone*," *four and five-eighths, thirty-hundredths, ninety-two thousandths*.

Do not use the hyphen in an instance as "*One half the business is owned by Mr. Jones, one quarter by Mr. Smith, and one eighth each by Mr. Browne and Mr. Robinson.*"

26. Where two or more compound words occur together having one of their components in common, this component is often omitted from all but the last word and the omission indicated by a hyphen;

> *French-and Spanish-speaking countries, wood-iron-and steel-work, one-two-three-four and five-cent stamps.*

> This usage is objected to in some offices as being a Germanized form. It is however, less ambiguous than where the hyphen is omitted and is therefore preferable.

27. Ordinal numbers compounded with nouns take the hyphen in such expressions as *second-hand, first-rate*, and the like.

28. Numerals of one syllable take a hyphen in compounds with self-explanatory words such as *four-footed, one-eyed*, and the like.

29. Numerals compounded with nouns to form an adjective take the hyphen; *twelve-inch rule, three-horse team, six-point lead*.

30. The hyphen is used in compounding a noun in the possessive case with another noun; *jew's-harp, crow's-nest*.

31. The hyphen is used with most compounds of *tree; apple-tree, quince-tree*, but not when a particular object, not a tree (vegetable), is meant; *whippletree, crosstree*.

32. Use the hyphen in compounding two adjectives generally, especially personal epithets; *asked-for opinion, sea-island cotton, dry-plate process, hard-headed, strong-armed, broad-shouldered*.

33. The hyphen is not used in points of the compass unless doubly compounded; *northeast, southwest, north-northeast, south-southwest by south*.

34. Compounds ending with *man* or *woman* are run solid; *pressman, forewoman.*

35. Omit the hyphen in such phrases as *by and by, by the bye, good morning* (except when used adjectively, *a good-morning greeting,*) *attorney at law, coat of arms.*

36. Compounds ending in *holder* and *monger* are run solid; *bondholder, cheesemonger.*

37. Compounds beginning with *eye* are run solid; *eyeglass, eyewitness.*

38. Compounds unless very unusual, beginning with *deutero, electro, pseudo, sulpho, thermo,* etc., are run solid; *electrotype, pseudonym, thermostat.*

39. Do not separate

meanwhile	*anywhere*	*somebody*
meantime	*anybody*	*somehow*
moreover	*anyhow*	*something*
forever	*anything*	*sometime*
everywhere	*anyway*	*somewhat*
	somewhere	

In phrases like *in the meantime* and *forever and ever* the words are printed separately.

Any one and *some one* are separate words.

40. In compounds of color the hyphen is not used except when a noun is used with an adjective to specify color; *reddish-brown, gray-white, lemon-yellow, olive-green, silver-gray.*

41. Following is a list of words of everyday occurrence which should be hyphenated, and which do not fall under any of the above classifications.

after-years	*food-stuff*	*sea-level*
bas-relief	*guinea-pig*	*sense-perception*
birth-rate	*horse-power*	*son-in-law*
blood-relations	*loan-word*	*subject-matter*
common-sense	*man-of-war*	*thought-process*
cross-examine	*object-lesson*	*title-page*
cross-reference	*page-proof*	*wave-length*
cross-section	*pay-roll*	*well-being*
death-rate	*poor-law*	*well-nigh*
folk-song	*post-office*	*will-power*
fountain-head		

These rules are the consensus of opinion of a considerable number of good authorities from DeVinne (1901) to Manly and Powell (1913). The great practical difficulty is that authorities differ as to their application. DeVinne uses the dieresis instead of the hyphen in such cases as *co-operate* or *pre-eminent*, writing *coöperate, preëminent*. Many of the rules have exceptions and authorities differ as to the extent of the exceptions. There are many differences in the great number of unclassified compounds. For example, Manly and Powell write *coat-of-arms*, while Orcutt writes *coat of arms*. Common usage omits the hyphen from post office except when used as an adjective, e. g., *post-office accounts*.

A strict adherence to the rules given would probably result, not in bad composition, but in a much greater use of hyphens than would be found on the pages of many recent books from the presses of some of the best publishers. This is due partly to the fact that usage has never been strictly uniform and partly to the constant progressive change noted at the beginning of this study. We are gradually discontinuing the use of the hyphen just as we are diminishing our use of capital letters, punctuation marks, and italics.

The compositor should ground himself thoroughly in the principles and rules. He should learn the best usage with regard to special words and phrases. He should master the office style. He should follow copy if the author has distinct and definite ideas which are not absolutely wrong and would not introduce inconsistencies in magazines and the like by violating the office style which is followed in other parts of the same publication. If it is clear that the author knows what he wants, the compositor should follow copy. Questions of correctness and conformity to style belong not to him but to the copy editor and proofreader.

SUPPLEMENTARY READING

English Compound Words and Phrases. By Francis Horace Teall. Funk & Wagnalls, New York.

The Compounding of English Words, When and Why Joining or Separation is Preferable. By Francis Horace Teall. J. Ireland, New York.

Correct Composition. By Theodore L. De Vinne. The Oswald Publishing Co., New York.

A Manual for Writers. By John Matthews Manly and John Arthur Powell. The University of Chicago Press, Chicago.

The Writer's Desk Book. By William Dana Orcutt. Frederick A. Stokes Co., New York.

REVIEW QUESTIONS

1. What is meant by a "compound"?
2. What is the purpose of a compound?
3. In what three forms do compounds appear?
4. Where should we expect to find guidance in the choice of these forms?
5. Do we so find it, and why?
6. What tendency is observable in usage regarding compounds?
7. What can the printer do?
8. Give Teall's rules, and show the application of each.
9. What is the influence of accent in compounding?
10. What is the rule about two nouns used together to form a name?
11. What is the rule about names composed of a plain noun and a verbal noun?
12. How are possessive phrases used as specific names treated?
13. What is the rule about phrases used as specific names?
14. How do you write a pair of words used as a name when the second word is a noun and the first not really an adjective?
15. How do you treat two words, not nouns, arbitrarily used as a name?
16. How do you treat a compound consisting of a suffix and a compound proper name?
17. How do you treat words so associated that their joint sense is different from their separate sense?
18. How may compounds having the force of nouns be made up?
19. How may compounds having the force of adjectives be made up?
20. How may compounds having the force of verbs be made up?
21. How may compounds having the force of adverbs be made up?
22. How are compound nouns written when one of the components is derived from a transitive verb?
23. How is a compound of a present participle and a noun written?
24. How is a compound of a present participle and a preposition treated?

25. What is the usage in compounds of *book, house, will, room, shop,* and *work*?
26. How are compounds of *maker* and *dealer* written?
27. What is done when nouns are combined in a descriptive phrase before a name of a person?
28. How are compounds of *store* treated?
29. How are compounds of *fellow* treated?
30. How are compounds of *father, mother, brother, sister, daughter, parent,* and *foster* treated?
31. What compounds of *great* are hyphenated?
32. How are compounds of *life* and *world* treated?
33. What is the rule about compounds of *skin*?
34. How are compounds of *master* treated?
35. What is the rule about compounds of *god*?
36. Give fifteen common prefixes and tell how they are used, stating exceptions.
37. What are the negative prefixes and how are they used?
38. What is the rule about the prefixes *quasi, extra, supra, ultra,* and *pan*?
39. What is the rule about *over* and *under*?
40. What is the rule about compounds of *self* and *by*?
41. How are compounds of *fold* treated?
42. What is the rule about compounds of a noun followed by *like*?
43. How are titles treated when compounded with *vice, elect, ex, general,* and *lieutenant*?
44. How do you write three familiar compounds denoting time?
45. How should you treat fractional numbers spelled out?
46. What is done when two or more compound words with a common component occur in succession?
47. How do you write compounds of ordinal numbers and nouns?
48. What rule is given about numerals of one syllable?
49. What rule is given about numerals compounded with nouns?
50. How do you treat a compound of two nouns one in the possessive case?
51. How are compounds of *tree* treated?
52. What is the rule about compounds of two adjectives?
53. What is the rule about points of the compass?
54. What should you do with compounds ending in *man* or *woman*?

55. Give certain common typical phrases which omit the hyphen.

56. How do you treat compounds ending in *holder* and *monger*?

57. How do you treat compounds beginning with *eye*?

58. What is said of compounds beginning with *deutero, electro, pseudo, sulpho, thermo,* and the like?

59. Give some common compounds which are always run solid.

60. How are compounds of color treated?

61. Are these rules universally followed?

62. What is the duty of the compositor in these cases, especially when doubtful?

In this volume, as in so many in this section, much depends upon practice drills. The memorizing of rules is difficult and is of very little use unless accompanied by a great deal of practice so that the apprentice will become so thoroughly familiar with them that he will apply them at once without conscious thought. He should no more think of the rule when he writes *fellow-man*, than he thinks of the multiplication table when he says seven times eight are fifty-six. This drill may be given in several ways, by asking the student to explain the use or omission of hyphens in printed matter, by giving written matter purposely incorrect in parts and asking him to set it correctly, or by giving dictations and having the apprentice write out the matter and then set it up. Later, when it will not be too wasteful of time, the apprentice can be given the ordinary run of copy as customers send it in and told to set it in correct form. He will probably find enough errors in it to test his knowledge of compounding and of many other things.

Lector House believes that a society develops through a two-fold approach of continuous learning and adaptation, which is derived from the study of classic literary works spread across the historic timeline of literature records. Therefore, we aim at reviving, repairing and redeveloping all those inaccessible or damaged but historically as well as culturally important literature across subjects so that the future generations may have an opportunity to study and learn from past works to embark upon a journey of creating a better future.

This book is a result of an effort made by Lector House towards making a contribution to the preservation and repair of original ancient works which might hold historical significance to the approach of continuous learning across subjects.

HAPPY READING & LEARNING!

LECTOR HOUSE LLP
E-MAIL: lectorpublishing@gmail.com